P9-DTY-727

794.6
C 1

BEGINNING
BOWLING

DONALD CASADY
State University of Iowa

MARIE LIBA
University of Wisconsin

WADSWORTH PUBLISHING COMPANY, INC.
Belmont, California

© 1962 by Wadsworth Publishing Company, Inc., Belmont, California. All rights reserved. No part of this book may be reproduced in any form, by mimeograph or any other means, without permission in writing from the publisher.

L.C. Cat. Card No.: 61-15832

Printed in the United States of America

CONTENTS

WITHDRAWN

630232

1

VALUES

Bowling is today one of the nation's most popular recreational activities. Almost every community, regardless of size, has a bowling establishment where individuals and league teams may bowl. At the present time, it is estimated that nearly 30,000,000 bowlers spend more than one billion dollars on bowling every year. By 1970, the number of bowlers is expected to increase to 40,000,000. Of all indoor sports, bowling is by far the most popular.

Bowling is a sport not reserved exclusively for the athlete. Elements of size, physical strength, and so on, have little influence on one's skill as a bowler. Nor is the enjoyment of the activity limited by the age or sex of the participant. People of all ages, children and senior citizens, men and women, can participate in this sport with a high degree of competence. Still, bowling demands enough physical activity to provide much of the exercise needed for maintaining good health. The need for and value of regular participation in some form of moderate exercise has been given a great deal of attention by scientific and medical authorities. Evidence gleaned from numerous studies indicates that there is a definite relationship between physical exercise and level of health, particularly the condition of the cardiovascular system. Thousands of workers in sedentary occupations find in bowling the means to get their much-needed exercise.

Physical exercise, however, is not all that bowling has to offer. The nature of the game demands that the participants be continually alert, and that their minds function from beginning to end with continued attention to matters of form, keeping score, and so on. Another and highly important benefit of the sport is that, as indicated by a recent study among league bowlers, it provides an opportunity to relax that is not found in less active forms of recreation. This is true whether one bowls alone or with other people. In bowling, one is continually competing with oneself, trying to improve one's score, as well as with the other members of a league team and

2

with the opposing teams. This kind of competitive spirit usually results in the kind of scores that gives the bowler the satisfaction that comes only through the skillful performance of a task.

More and more in recent years, bowling lanes have become a place where one can enjoy recreation with both friends and family. Bowling proprietors have placed increasing emphasis on convenience and comfort in an attempt to provide pleasant and wholesome surroundings. This has been the stimulus for the very popular "family bowling," and has been an important influence on the increased participation of women and children in the sport. The bowling establishment, since it has become so popular in recent years, is a fine place to get together with old friends for a casual game, as well as a place where one can make new friends through participation in leagues and other activities.

630232

2 HISTORY

The game of bowling has been one of man's recreational pursuits since the beginning of the recorded history of mankind. Bowling games have developed in various areas of the world, and at the present time many variations exist.

THE BEGINNING OF BOWLING

Artifacts of the Stone Age indicate that the primitive people of Europe played a type of bowling game in which large pebbles or rocks were rolled at pointed stones or the bones of animals. There is evidence that the ancient Polynesians had a bowling game, called *Ula Maika*, in which rounded stones were rolled at flat stone discs.

Bowling implements were discovered by Sir Flinders Petrie, an Egyptologist, in the tomb of an Egyptian boy estimated by archaeologists to have lived in 5200 B.C. In this game, the Egyptians used stone balls which were rolled at marble bars, slabs of stone, or pottery.

The Romans in what is now northern Italy are known to have engaged in a form of bowling as early as 50 B.C. The Roman bowling game was quite similar to the present Italian lawn-bowling game of *Bocce Ball* and is credited as being the forerunner of today's lawn-bowling games.

BOWLING IN EUROPE

Records written around 300 A.D. indicate that the modern game of *Tenpins* may have originated in central European monasteries and cathedrals as part of a religious ritual where the parishioners, while attending church, rolled a large stone or ball at a wooden club placed in a corner. The canons (clerics) are said to have told the parishioners that the club symbolically represented evil or the devil. Thus, if the club was hit with the ball, the parishioner received praise from the canon for leading a good life, however, if the club was

4

missed, he was told to lead a better life. The clerics soon became interested in the idea of hitting the club with a ball and subsequently developed a bowling game called *Kegel*. Others also desired to try their kegeling skill and, hence, the game of bowling at a single pin spread. Still later, additional pins were added and as the game gained popularity people of nobility and wealth took up the game.

Variations of this and other bowling games spread throughout Europe. Various kinds of pin bowling games were popular in Germany, Holland, and Switzerland during the Middle Ages. These games were at first played outdoors on grass, later on clay alleys, and by 1200 A.D. the ball was rolled down a single wooden board 12–18 inches in width, which was placed on the clay alleys. In time, covered sheds were built over the alleys, and still later wooden indoor alleys were built. A great diversification existed in the pin bowling games of that era. Pins and balls differed widely in size and weight and were employed in games in which from three to seventeen pins were used. Martin Luther is credited with fixing the number of pins at nine and standardizing the rules of the game of *Ninepins*.

During the sixteenth century, bowling games enjoyed great popularity throughout Europe. The French played a pin-bowling game called *Quilles* and a game similar to lawn bowling called *Garreau*. In Scotland, the national bowling game was *Curling* (played on ice) which was adapted from a bowling game played by the Flemish people. Different bowling games at this time included *Skittles*, *Half-bowl*, *Basque*, *Bowls*, *Shovelboard* (now called *Shuffleboard*) and *Ninepins*, which was the favorite bowling game in Holland.

BOWLING IN AMERICA

In the 1620's, the game of Ninepins was brought by the Dutch settlers to Manhattan when the island was first inhabited by Europeans. Although lawn bowling had a measure of popularity, pin bowling spread until it was popular in many sections of the Eastern United States, particularly with the German immigrants. Ninepins probably attained its peak of popularity by 1840; the first bowling house was built in New York City during that year.

Because of the heavy wagering on the outcome of bowling matches, bowling gradually became controlled by gamblers. For this reason, the game of Ninepins was outlawed first in Connecticut in 1841 and later in New York, Massachusetts, and other Eastern states. The game of Tenpins, in which an extra pin was added to the nine pins, thus circumventing the law prohibiting Ninepin bowling, began to attain popularity during the 1840's. In Tenpins, the pins were arranged in a triangular formation instead of the diamond formation used in Ninepins.

Tenpins soon became popular over much of the country, but there were many variations in the rules, size of pins, size of alleys, and size of bowling balls. Consequently, the National Bowling Congress was organized in 1875 for the purpose of standardizing the rules of the game. This organization soon ceased to function and in 1890 the American Amateur Bowling Union was formed but soon went out of existence. Finally, in order to allow all bowlers in the United States to bowl under standardized conditions, the American Bowling Congress (ABC) was formed in 1895. The ABC was also given the task of establishing national rules and regulations, promoting bowling, formulating specifications for bowling equipment and bowling alleys, and supervising bowling in the United States. The ABC remains as the main governing body for organized bowling in this country. The Women's International Bowling Congress was established in 1916, and the American High School Bowling Congress was established soon afterwards.

DEVELOPMENT OF BOWLING FACILITIES
AND EQUIPMENT

As the game of bowling has changed, so have bowling establishments evolved and grown. From buildings containing two to six alleys, which were used primarily by men and which were considered places of evil since gambling was rampant, bowling establishments have evolved into large structures containing as many as 100 alleys and in which entire families bowl.

Bowling pins have also undergone a considerable evolution in shape and size. Originally, pins were wooden clubs that tapered toward the top. Later, small cones varying in length and diameter were used, and these were replaced by small keg-shaped pins, flat on the bottom and top. Eventually, the shape of the champagne bottle was adopted as the standard shape for bowling pins.

In a similar manner, bowling balls have changed. Thousands of years ago, small round stones served as bowling balls. Later, wooden balls were used; then rubber balls were tried. Still later, wooden balls that were smooth-surfaced and truly round in shape were turned out on power lathes. Shortly before the advent of the twentieth century, hard-rubber composition balls with two-finger grips were introduced into the United States.

The change in specifications for alley beds ranges from the level grassy areas first used in primitive outdoor games to the present wooden alley beds where a maximum levelness tolerance of .040 inch is permitted.

While Tenpins attracts by far the greatest number of bowling participants in the United States, other bowling games including such "small-ball games" as Duck Pins, Candle Pins, Five Pins, and Rubber-band Duck Pins are popular in some sections of the country. In these games the bowling ball is about 5 inches in diameter and is carried in the palm of the hand during the delivery.

EQUIPMENT

One reason for the popularity of bowling is that no special equipment need be purchased by the beginner since bowling establishments rent bowling shoes for a minimum amount and the use of bowling balls, pins, and the alley is included in the bowling fee. The dimensions of the lanes, pins, and ball are standardized; thus, the beginning bowler is not concerned with making a decision about various sizes of equipment. The standard dimensions of a bowling alley, ball, and pin are shown in Illustration 1.

Dress and Shoes

Loose, comfortable clothing that allows freedom of movement and is acceptable in the community should be the attire when bowling. Stylish clothing made of a variety of materials and designed specifically for bowling may be obtained by both men and women. The person who bowls frequently will probably wish to purchase bowling shoes, since this will result in a saving for him. Right-handed bowlers should get shoes with a leather sole on the left shoe (to facilitate the slide on the last step) and a rubber sole on the right shoe. Leather bowling shoes come in a variety of styles and colors and cost from $5.00 to $15.00.

SELECTION OF BOWLING BALL

Advanced bowlers usually purchase a custom-fitted ball even though bowling establishments provide an assortment of house balls. The bowling balls provided by a bowling establishment do not always give a perfect fit, however, and often it is difficult for bowlers with short, compact hands or with long, narrow hands to find a comfortable-fitting house ball. There are enough problems on which the beginning or even advanced bowler must concentrate when bowling without adding the problem presented by using a poorly-fitted bowling ball.

Dimensions of bowling equipment

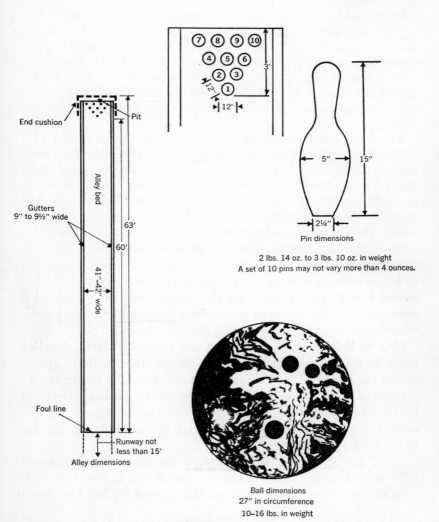

End cushion

Pit

Alley bed

Gutters
9" to 9½" wide

63'

60'

41"–42" wide

Foul line

Runway not
less than 15'

Alley dimensions

7 8 9 10
4 5 6
2 3
1

3'

12"

12"

5"

15"

2¼"

Pin dimensions

2 lbs. 14 oz. to 3 lbs. 10 oz. in weight
A set of 10 pins may not vary more than 4 ounces.

Ball dimensions
27" in circumference
10–16 lbs. in weight

Illustration 1

Such factors as body weight, over-all strength, strength of the grip, size of the hand, and the speed of the delivery should all play a role in determining the ball best suited for each bowler. A ball should be selected that can be gripped and swung without excessive strain.

Weight of Bowling Ball. Two opposing variables must be counterbalanced in selecting a bowling ball of the correct weight. First, the heavier the ball, the more efficiently will it knock down pins, since a heavier ball exerts more force against the pins than does a lighter one. Second, the lighter the ball, the faster it can be delivered with control; up to a certain speed, the faster ball gives better pin action.

The main consideration in determining the correct weight of a ball is the bowler's ability to handle the given weight. The bowling ball selected should be no heavier than that weight which allows the ball to be delivered without unnecessary strain, with consistency, and with accuracy. The beginner is urged to select a light-weight ball that can be easily handled. Should the right shoulder drop appreciably during the delivery, or should the ball be prematurely released a number of times, then too heavy a ball is probably being used.

In general, women use bowling balls that vary in weight from ten to fifteen pounds; while a few women use a sixteen-pound ball, that weight is not recommended for the average woman bowler. Men generally use balls varying in weight from fourteen to sixteen pounds with the sixteen-pound ball most commonly chosen.

Grip of Ball. A poorly-fitting ball can adversely affect a bowling game by many pins. Worse, it often causes other faults to appear during the approach and delivery. For this reason, the serious bowler is urged to purchase a custom-fitted ball as soon as he has determined his choice of weight and grip. The size and type of grip selected depends upon the strength of grip, the span of the hand, and the size of the fingers and thumb.

Span. The span or distance between the finger and the thumb holes should be such that when the regular grip is used * there is sufficient space between the ball and the palm of the hand to snugly

* Thumb inserted from about three-fourths to its full length, according to the bowler's preference, and the middle and ring fingers inserted to a distance between the first and second joints but closer to the second joint.

insert a pencil or the little finger of the non-bowling hand, while the ball is supported on the rack or another surface. Another method of fitting the span is to take a regular grip on the ball and then, while holding the thumb in place with the other hand, withdraw the fingers and hold them extended over the finger holes. The fleshy folds or the creases of the first joints on the back of the fingers should extend one-fourth to one-half of the distance between the inside lips of the finger holes and the outside lips.

Too short a span fatigues the hand, because the ball must be gripped tighter than is necessary on a properly fitted ball; too long a span is uncomfortable and causes increased strain and fatigue, since, unless the hand is unduly extended, the fingers cannot be fully bent at the second joints.

Size of Holes. A proper fit of the span makes tight-fitting thumb or finger holes unnecessary. The finger and thumb holes should be of sufficient diameter so that the thumb and particularly the fingers can move in and out of the holes freely, with little or no friction. The holes should never fit so tight that there is a "glub" or a "pop" when the thumb or fingers leave the holes on the release. In the thumb hole, some friction may be present at the sides of the thumb or when the thumb is bent but the thumb hole should fit more loosely than the finger holes. Stated in another fashion, the holes should be loose enough for comfort but small enough to provide a strong grip. During the delivery, the ball tends to be dropped too soon if the holes are too large; and the ball may be "lofted" (that is, thrown out on the alley bed a few feet beyond the foul line) if the holes are too small.

Pitch of Holes. The pitch of a hole is determined by the angle formed by the axis of the hole toward the center of the ball. The thumb and finger holes would intersect at three-eighths of an inch above the center of the ball on a three-eighths inward pitch, which is the standard pitch bored in most balls. Other common pitches are the inward one-quarter and inward one-half pitches, although some balls have no pitch or even a reverse pitch in which the axis of the holes intersect on the far side of the center of the ball. Bowlers with wide hand spans sometimes use a reverse pitch. The weaker the grasp, the more inward pitch required in order to assure a firm grip when delivering the ball. The thumb hole can be bored at a greater or lesser pitch than the finger holes are bored in order to meet individual preference.

In addition to regular pitch, the finger holes of some balls are bored with a side pitch in which the axes of the holes pass to one side of the center of the ball.

Number of Finger Holes. The most popular type of bowling ball in use today is the three-hole ball in which the thumb, middle finger, and ring finger are inserted in the three holes.

Fingertip Balls. Bowling balls with a semi-fingertip, a fingertip, or a combination of a regular and a fingertip grip are favored by some advanced bowlers.

Cost of Bowling Ball and Bag. Custom-fitted bowling balls are generally sold in those stores that handle other bowling equipment. Most bowling balls cost from $24.00 to $30.00. Bowling establishments usually have ball cleaning machines that quickly clean and polish the bowling ball for a small charge. Bowling bags for transporting the ball, and sometimes the shoes, range in cost from $4.00 to $10.00 in plastic or cotton, or from $10.00 to $30.00 for good quality leather bags.

Selection of Equipment. Once the fundamental skills of bowling have been mastered, the beginner should determine his enthusiasm and probable future participation in the game. Then, the amount and the quality of special bowling equipment to be purchased can be decided. The sale of bowling equipment is sufficiently competitive to insure that the quality of the equipment improves as the price increases.

TECHNIQUES OF PARTICIPATION 4

The techniques that comprise the *fundamental skills* of the game of bowling are presented in this chapter. A mastery of these should be the goal of every beginner since they will enable him to develop his own skill in bowling. Proper instruction and its correct application are important, however, if the beginning bowler is to master these fundamentals. Practice of the correct bowling fundamentals by beginners usually results in definite and rapid improvement, whereas practicing incorrectly is of little value.

Information about recommended methods of practicing bowling skills may be obtained by studying this booklet, but, since most persons have at best only a hazy concept of what they actually do when bowling, instruction by a qualified instructor is likely to be necessary. A bowling instructor can also help ensure that the beginning bowler accurately carries out his instructions. When an improper action is performed, he can immediately suggest corrections and, thus, the beginner avoids developing bad habits that are difficult to eliminate.

Many different styles of bowling are utilized by the star bowlers who often appear on television bowling programs. Although these star bowlers may have faults in their deliveries, they are successful because they spend many hours weekly in practicing. Since there is no one way to bowl, the form or bowling style of a star bowler should not be imitated, but the beginner should develop his own natural style.

It is equally important that a beginner making use of these fundamentals find time for a considerable amount of practice and diligent effort in delivering the ball before the end result of consistent success in knocking down pins can be achieved. Here bowling instructors again and again point out the importance of careful attention to the development of the arm swing and the approach, the coordination of these two, and the importance of performing these consistently, with little or no variation, before undue emphasis is given to knocking

13

down pins. The beginner is advised always to concentrate on each delivery of the ball; a rapid improvement in skill requires concentration at all times.

The fundamental skills will first be described in the sequence in which they would appear in the coordinated ball delivery. The succeeding chapter will be devoted to a discussion of how the fundamental skills can be practiced and incorporated into the coordinated arm swing and approach.

In this booklet, the techniques of bowling are presented for right-handed bowlers. Left-handed bowlers must reverse the directions.

STANCE

The stance is the position assumed by the bowler preparatory to delivering the ball. It should be comfortable, because it is the foundation for the approach and delivery. A variety of stances may be used. The beginner should experiment with several stance positions until a suitable one is found. Regardless of the final position chosen, certain rules should be observed.

Grip on Ball. While in the stance, the bowling arm and hand will become less fatigued if the weight of the ball is supported by the non-bowling hand. The thumb and the fingers of the bowling hand should be placed in the holes of the ball and relaxed. The position of the little finger and the forefinger when gripping the three-hole ball may vary; the position used depends on individual preference. The two most popular positions are with the fingers touching (compact grip) and with the little finger and the index finger spread (the natural grip which is the type most commonly used).

Position of Ball. Some right-handed bowlers center the ball in front of the right shoulder during the stance since this position is conducive to a pendular swing and aids in eliminating any tendency to side-arm the ball. In this position, the ball swing can be started in a straight arc forward and backward, which is an advantage in achieving a consistent release position. For those beginning bowlers, particularly women, who have difficulty with their plane of swing and tend to side-arm the ball during the delivery, it is suggested that the ball be held in front of the right shoulder during the stance.

Other beginning bowlers will wish to hold the ball in front of the center of the body during the stance. In this position, the ball can be supported with relative ease by both arms, and it can be aimed at the target while being pushed away from the body.

During the stance, the ball may be positioned at any height from knee level to eye level. The range of positions commonly used are from hip level to chin level with the waist-to-chest-height range recommended for most beginners.

Position of Body. It is important that the target be squarely faced while the bowler is in the stance. In this position, the lines formed by the shoulders and hips are parallel with the foul line. The body position when in the stance may range from an upright position to one in which the body is in low crouch with the trunk at a right angle to the legs. The recommended position is one in which there is a slight bend at the waist and in which comfort and relaxation are stressed.

Position of Feet. The position of the feet during the stance depends upon the number of steps in the approach and the general inclination. A common position is one with the feet in line and spread apart a few inches. However, many bowlers often stand with the foot that takes the first step a few inches behind the other foot. A few bowlers reverse this position. The legs are often slightly bent at the knee joints in order to promote relaxation and to facilitate the leg bend during delivery. The body weight often primarily rests on the foot that does *not* take the first step forward in the approach.

The beginner is urged to experiment with various stances until he finds one that is comfortable and natural for him. Once this stance

Illustration 2

has been established, it should be permanently adopted. In Illustration 2, two front views and three side views of stances commonly used in bowling are shown.

APPROACH

The approach encompasses the movements made toward the foul line when delivering the bowling ball. It is the foundation for an accurate, effective delivery that requires no unnecessary muscular effort. Considerable variation is evident in the approaches used by champion bowlers and in the approaches taught by bowling instructors, but the movements of the body should reflect a utilization of physical principles if effective deliveries are to be made. Therefore, these principles must be observed during the approach if the delivery is to be consistently successful. The footwork utilized in the approach is an important phase of bowling for the beginner, because in order to achieve a consistent delivery, he must coordinate his footwork with his arm swing.

Direction of the Approach. The starting and finishing position in relation to the side of the runway must always be the same in order to have a consistent release position at the foul line. The "strike" ball (the first ball delivered in each frame) should be released at exactly the same position at the foul line on every delivery. One of the most significant aspects of effective bowling is that *the steps in the approach should be made in a straight line toward and perpendicular to the foul line.* If this can be achieved, and it is somewhat more difficult than it appears, considerably less difficulty will be encountered in establishing a consistent release position for the strike ball.

Speed of the Approach. The approach should never be hurried. Beginners, especially men, often make the mistake of rushing the approach and, consequently, have completed it before the ball is in position for the release. Poor timing and inaccuracy result. On the other hand, particularly for women, the approach should not be too deliberate but should accelerate from the first to the last step. Otherwise, the approach adds little to the bowler's momentum and is of little value in the delivery of the ball.

The steps in the approach can best be described as a walk and each succeeding one should be slightly longer than the preceding one.

This provides the opportunity to develop momentum during the approach to the foul line. Momentum can also be generated by progressively increasing the speed of each successive step or by both lengthening and speeding each successive step. In the last analysis, when delivering the ball, the bowler should strive to use his natural speed; this varies with the bowler's height, strength, speed of approach, number of steps, and the type of delivery used.

Length of Approach. The "runway" or approach area is at least fifteen feet long and it is generally advisable to utilize as much of the runway as possible. A lengthy approach enables sufficient momentum to be developed during the approach without exerting undue effort. To determine the correct starting distance, stand with the heels next to the foul line and face away from the pins. Then execute a regular delivery but without releasing the ball. By adding approximately six inches to the finish position, the spot from which to begin the approach is located. Another system sometimes used to determine the starting position is to start from the foul line with the back to the pins and then walk in a normal fashion, taking the same number of steps as used in the delivery. To this finish position another half step is added, and this spot is used as the location from which to begin the delivery.

An approach ending with the left foot just short of the foul line after the slide in the last step is completed is of the correct length. Once the starting spot has been determined, always begin the delivery from exactly the same spot. Mark this spot by utilizing the dots of the Brunswick Range Finder or by measuring the distance from the back of the approach area. The importance of observing this should not be underestimated.

The Arm Swing. It has already been pointed out and will be mentioned again that the key to good bowling is consistency. Since the arm swing is the method of applying force and direction to the ball, its importance cannot be overemphasized. The arm movement or swing is critical since a correctly executed arm swing is essential in providing the proper ball delivery. It should be emphasized that the arm swing can be modified by changes in the body position or in the approach. Thus, all aspects of the approach are necessary, but without a consistent arm swing with the correct mechanics of movement, the beginning bowler can never achieve a consistent delivery.

Pendular Swing. The entire arm swing during the approach is a pendular swing such as is described by the pendulum of a grandfather clock. The pendular swing appears to be of outstanding importance in achieving accuracy in bowling. To do it, first let the ball hang, keeping the bowling arm straight at all times, then lift the ball forward and upward, allowing the weight of the ball to carry it down-

PUSHAWAY AND BACKSWING

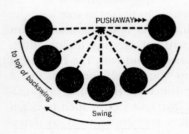

PUSHAWAY▸▸▸

to top of backswing

Swing

FORWARD MOTION AND RELEASE

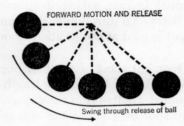

Swing through release of ball

Illustration 3

ward. The ball will continue to travel backward in the backswing due to inertia. Gravity and then inertia again causes the downward swing in a forward direction. When done correctly, the motion of the ball closely resembles the swing of a pendulum. While inertia and gravity aid the pendular swing, the bowler must push the ball outward and he aids the back swing and the forward swing as needed for the release. The beginner should avoid allowing the right shoulder to drop excessively when the ball swings downward. Beginners are urged to practice a pendular swing from a standing position until they get the correct feel of this type of swing. Note the use of the word *swing*. This term is important in interpret-

ing what the movement of the arm is like as it moves in an arc in a vertical plane. The ball should swing freely and not be carried or thrown. The motion of the pendular swing is shown in Illustration 3.

Pushaway. The arm swing in the approach is initiated by pushing the ball forward; this movement is called the pushaway. This is an appropriate term in that it suggests a push forward of the ball, not merely a dropping or a lowering of the ball into motion. On the pushaway, in order to align the swing of the arm with the target, the ball is directed toward the target until the bowling arm is almost or completely extended. The pushaway should take the ball forward as far as or farther than the length of the first step. On all pushaways, the non-bowling hand assists in pushing the ball away from the body. It is recommended that the bowling arm *not* be bent after the push-away has been completed.

Backswing. The concept of the swinging motion of the arm immediately raises the question of the range of the arm movement in the backswing. Unless the range of the arm movement is relatively large, the concept of the pendular swing is lost. Here again there is no one position that is best. The amount and the height of the back swing vary according to the bowler's arm strength, the weight of the ball, the height of the ball at the completion of the pushaway, the erectness of the bowler's body, and the force of the arm swing. However, observation of a great many bowlers indicates that the most common position at the end of the backswing is one in which the arm is almost parallel to the floor (see Illustration 3). This seems most reasonable since this range of movement enables the ball to be swung freely. The right shoulder should never markedly go backward because of the backswing of the ball.

Forward Swing. The ball should not be snapped forward or the bowling arm bent at the elbow during the forward arm swing. Instead, the arm should feel like a rope from the shoulder to the ball. The ball should never be side-armed on either the backward or the forward arm swing. Side-arming the ball can be avoided by maintaining a pendular swing, by correctly timing the delivery with the steps, by keeping the shoulders square to the foul line, and by keeping the ball directly in line with the shoulder of the bowling arm.

Timing of the Arm Swing and Approach. Speaking for the right-handed bowler—the left foot and the right arm must be coming forward at the same time on the last step. This is the goal in developing coordination or timing of the arm swing and the approach. A good start which includes the pushaway—and a pushaway that will more or less pull the bowler forward into the approach—is the best assurance that the arm swing and steps will be properly timed. Then, if the approach is not unduly slowed down or rushed and if the range and swing of the arm are maintained, the left foot and right arm will be coming forward together on the last step. One check point might be mentioned. Regardless of the number of steps taken, the height of the backswing is reached as the last step with the right foot is taken. The proper coordination of the bowling arm and the footwork during the approach is essential in order to insure an accurate delivery. In a delivery of normal speed, however, the position of the bowling arm *cannot* be exactly determined during each step. In the final analysis, the bowler must depend upon the ease of the delivery and release in order to determine if the approach and arm swing were correctly timed.

Release of the Ball. The ball should be released after the ball has passed the forward foot and as the forward swing starts upward. Reach forward during the release so that the ball lands on the alley from one to two feet in front of the foul line. Reaching forward on the release eliminates a tendency to drop or loft the ball on the delivery. Men bowlers should avoid a tendency to throw the ball during the release; instead they should continue the normal arm swing.

The Follow-Through. The bowling hand should follow through freely and may go as high as the head on the follow-through. It is essential that the delivery of the ball be completed with a full follow-through of the bowling arm in order to prevent slowing the arm before the release and losing the swinging characteristic of the arm movement. Failure to observe this rule may result in the ball being "carried"—a common fault of women bowlers during the release. While it is true that any action performed after the release of the ball does *not* affect the path of the ball, the lack of a follow-through tends to encourage a faulty release and to cause errors to be committed before the release is made. A smooth release may be obtained by rolling rather than throwing the ball on the alley.

Position of the Body. It has already been pointed out that the arm swing is the most important factor in good bowling, but that other parts of the body may disrupt a good arm swing. The bowler should face the pins squarely during the arm swing and the release. If the spine is rotated or twisted, the shoulders will *not* be square with the target and a loss of the straight forward and backward swing of the arm may result. At the time the ball is released, the square position of the shoulders to the foul line is essential for the ball to be delivered in the desired line.

The body often leans forward slightly during the delivery in order to facilitate the development of momentum in the approach. A forward body lean also permits an increase in the range of the backswing.

During the release, the body is bent somewhat at the waist and the knees and the hips are kept low. Since the bowler has quite a bit of momentum during his delivery, this low release position will allow him to stop behind the foul line without a jerky movement. The upper part of the body will tend to carry forward and no effort should be made to stop its movement abruptly.

The foot opposite the bowling arm should finish from two to six inches behind the foul line and should point directly at the target. For righthanded bowlers, the right foot should finish behind the body. For increased ball control and body balance, the right foot should stay in contact with the alley bed during the release and the follow-through. The non-bowling arm is usually carried straight out from the side as an aid in maintaining balance at the completion of the approach and release.

The position of the bowler after releasing the first ball of a frame (strike ball) should always be the same and should be directly in front of the starting position and in line with the target. The novice bowler should form the habit of checking his position after each release in order to determine if his body and arm are pointing toward the target and if he is in the correct release position.

NUMBER OF STEPS TO USE

One of the first questions arising in consideration of the approach is how many steps to use. When first learning the approach and delivery, beginning bowlers may use a one-step or a two-step approach, but these should be considered as groundwork to an approach involving four or five steps. The four-step approach is the most popular approach used by present-day bowlers; however, the five-step approach is also recommended and is used by many star bowlers. The three-step approach is sometimes used but it is not generally recommended because it requires a disproportionate amount of effort by the bowling arm.

The length of the approach and the number of steps used depends to some extent on the type of body build and the height. The three-step approach is recommended for those people who have difficulty in timing their footwork with the delivery of the ball or who possess muscular coordination not easily adaptable to more than a three-step delivery. A tall person often uses a four-step or in some cases even a three-step approach since his long steps may carry him past the foul line if he utilizes a five-step approach.

Bowlers who are short in stature or who are somewhat weak in strength generally use a four- or a five-step approach since they need more steps in which to generate a delivery of adequate speed without over-reliance on arm strength. The five-step delivery is also used by bowlers preferring to take the first step with the left foot or desiring to use short steps.

The beginner is advised to experiment with both the four- and five-step approaches, if time permits, and then to use the approach which he finds to be best suited to his needs and abilities. The important point is to choose the approach that can be easily coordinated with the arm swing. The timing of the arm swing and the approach depends not only upon the number of steps taken, but the timing is affected by the height and length of the pushaway, the height of the backswing, the speed of the entire arm swing, and the length and speed of the approach. Consequently, the timing of the armswing and approach is an individual matter varying with each bowler. As a general guide, in the three-step approach the pushaway is usually completed and the downswing started before the first step begins; in the four-step approach either the pushaway or the downswing may begin simultaneously with the first step; and in the five-step approach the pushaway sometimes begins after the first step is completed.

Four-step Approach

The four-step approach is usually started from twelve to fifteen feet behind the foul line, but this distance varies for each individual. The first step should be somewhat slow, relatively short, and a natural walking step. Usually, as the first step begins, the ball is pushed with both hands to arms' length or nearly so. However, some bowlers do not begin their first step until the downswing is started.

The second step, taken with the left foot, is almost normal in length and speed. By the completion of the second step, the ball has dropped downward to its lowest point and is beside or slightly behind the body.

The third step is longer and faster than a normal stride. The

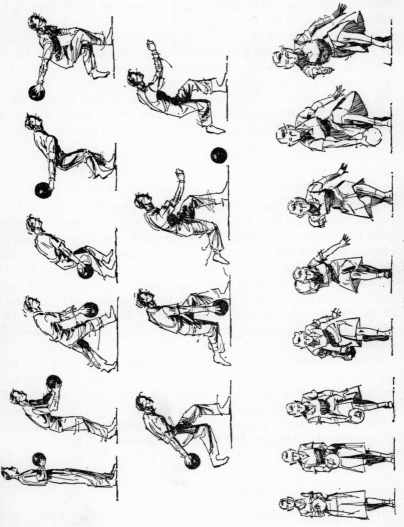

Illustration 4

bowling arm swings to or slightly past the peak of the backswing by the completion of the third step.

The fourth and last step is a long, gliding stride, which terminates in a slide by the left foot that may vary in length from a few inches to two feet. The ball must start downward and forward as the last step is initiated in order for the ball to be in position for the release as the slide is completed. The bowler should be in good balance when he releases the ball since this indicates that proper timing was used, thus assuring an accurate delivery. The four-step approach is shown in Illustration 4.

Five-step Approach

The five-step approach is usually started about fifteen feet behind the foul line. The first step is quite short and is primarily used to start the bowler in motion. In the five-step approach, the bowler often carries the ball in the stance position during the first step and then pushes the ball forward during the second step. At the end of the third step the ball is at the bottom point of the downswing, and at the completion of the fourth step the ball is at the highest point of the backswing. The ball is delivered at the completion of the fifth step as is done during the last step of the three- and four-step delivery.

Other five-step bowlers time the approach by pushing the ball forward as the first step is initiated. With this timing, the next three steps are utilized to carry the ball into a full backswing, and the ball is swung forward and released during the fifth step. The backswing tends to be higher in this style of the five-step approach than when the pushaway is delayed until the second step is started.

TYPES OF DELIVERIES

The type of ball delivery refers to the path followed by the ball when rolling down the lane. The two general types of deliveries are the straight-ball delivery and the curve-ball delivery. According to the type of curve described by the ball, curve-ball deliveries are divided into three sub-types: the hook-ball delivery, the curve-ball delivery,

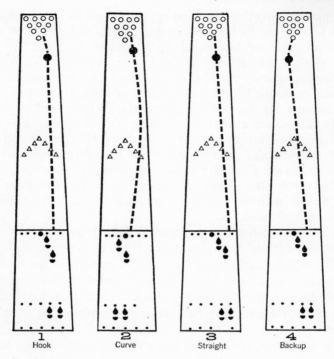

Types of ball deliveries

Illustration 5

and the backup-ball delivery. The last two are generally not recommended. The four types of deliveries are shown in Illustration 5.

WHAT TYPE OF DELIVERY TO USE

The beginner should carefully weigh the advantages and disadvantages of the hook ball and the straight ball before deciding which of the two types he prefers. In two studies of the hook-ball delivery versus the straight-ball delivery, the average scores of beginning women bowlers was the same regardless of the type of delivery used. Once a type of delivery has been chosen, the beginner should practice only this type. The beginner should select the delivery that is best suited to his abilities and needs, and not copy some champion bowler just because his style looks good.

The straight-ball delivery is frequently advocated by bowling authorities as an easy type that is best suited for casual bowlers who bowl only occasionally and who practice infrequently if at all. This is true because the straight-ball delivery can be controlled more consistently than can the hook-ball delivery. When bowling at spares, the straight ball is accurate and is easily aimed. However, the straight ball has a low strike percentage since it is deflected quite readily when it strikes the pins. The other disadvantage of a straight ball is that a relatively strong grasp is required since the thumb is in a twelve o'clock position, which is a somewhat unnatural position of the forearm and hand.

The hook-ball delivery is recommended for those who take their bowling seriously and who plan to practice with some regularity. As compared to the straight-ball delivery, the advantages of the hook-ball delivery are that the ball has a low degree of deflection due to its relatively large right-to-left angle just before contacting the pins, and that it is a strike-producing ball because it imparts spin or mix to the pins.

One disadvantage of the hook ball occurs when the second ball in a frame (spare shot) is delivered from a different position on the runway and, hence, the ball is delivered at a different angle than the one normally used for the first-ball delivery. This complicates the aim (especially for inexperienced bowlers) because the amount of hook on the ball depends in part on the angle of the delivery. Another complicating factor of the hook-ball is that some alleys are slower than others (on a slow alley the ball readily grips the alley bed and, consequently, curves more than would be normal). This factor requires the bowler to experiment with his first two or three deliveries in order to determine how much of a hook his delivery is producing on that alley. In league or championship bowling, he has to determine this for two alleys. After determining the slickness of the alley, the hook-ball bowler may have to adjust his aim, the amount of hook on the ball, or his starting position on the runway. Despite these complications, the hook-ball delivery is used by practically all star bowlers and, when controlled, is considered a better strike-getter than the straight ball.

Straight-ball Delivery

For the straight-ball delivery, the bowler should begin his approach from the right-hand corner of the approach with his left foot at a position five to ten boards in from the right-hand gutter. When gripping the ball for a straight-ball delivery, it is recommended that the thumb be held in the twelve o'clock position, although this may vary from ten to two o'clock. The thumb should be maintained in this position throughout the arm swing and release, and there should be no rotation of the forearm during the arm swing and delivery. The thumb comes out first during the release of the ball. The fingers leave the ball last and, since they are underneath the ball, they give a final lift which imparts an upward spin so that the ball rotates on an axis parallel with the foul line. A straight-ball delivery is depicted in Illustration 6.

Illustration 6

Hook-ball Delivery

The approach for the hook-ball delivery is from ten to fifteen boards (inside ¾ angle) in from the right-hand side of the approach. The distance from the side varies somewhat according to the amount of break or hook that the ball takes. In the hook-ball delivery, the thumb should come out first in order to allow the fingers to come out last and impart an upward motion to one side of the ball. Therefore, for a consistent hooking action, the hook-ball bowler needs a good follow-through and a ball with a relatively loose thumb hole.

While a hook ball may be rolled at about any speed, it is usually bowled at a slower speed than the straight ball. The more speed used in the delivery of the hook ball, the less it will hook. Four different techniques are used to produce the hooking action of the ball during the release.

Natural-hook Delivery. The simplest method of hooking the ball and one that produces accurate ball control is the natural-hook delivery. In this method the ball is carried with the thumb in the nine o'clock position and with the fingers in the three o'clock position. The "V" formed by the thumb on the left and the fingers on the right is in a horizontal plane as in a hand-shaking position, and the "V" points toward the pins or the ceiling above the pins. The position of the bowling hand should be maintained throughout the approach and release so that the "V" points at the target after the release has been made. The natural hook-ball delivery is depicted in Illustration 7.

Forced or Wrist-hook Delivery. In order to secure an increased hook on the ball, some bowlers rotate their forearm in a counter-

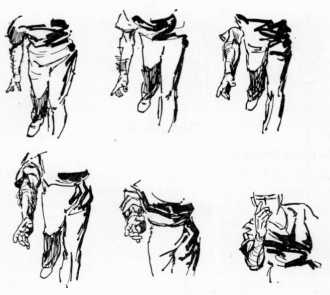

Illustration 7

clockwise direction as they release the ball. This method of hooking the ball is called the forced- or wrist-hook. Several variations exist, all of which involve only a rotation of the forearm. To bowl a wrist-hook delivery, the ball should be gripped in approximately the same position as is used for the natural hook although the thumb position can range from eight to eleven o'clock. As the ball leaves the hand on the release, the thumb is, by forearm rotation, turned from right to left to a finish position of from five to seven o'clock.

Lift-hook or Straight-lift Hook Delivery. Another method of securing increased hooking action is to forcefully lift the fingers upward when releasing the ball. In this method, the hand is almost directly underneath the ball, and the thumb is at about the ten or eleven o'clock position. The hand remains in the same position throughout the delivery but the fingers leave the ball last and lift vigorously in order to impart a counter-clockwise spin to the ball. Of the four hook-types of deliveries, the lift hook probably permits the best ball control.

Lift-and-turn Hook Delivery. The most hook-producing method of of the four is to rotate the forearm, counter-clockwise, and at the same time forcefully lift the fingers as the ball is being released. This combination method puts the maximum amount of hooking action on the ball because the finger lift and the forearm rotation both contribute to the spin on the ball. The lift-and-turn hook is the most difficult of all the hook balls to control, and it is the hook delivery with the most variations. Again the thumb, at the beginning of the approach, is in approximately the eleven o'clock position, and the thumb finishes at about the six o'clock position. Because of its effective pin action, the lift-and-turn hook is used by most star bowlers who often practice several hours daily in order to maintain a consistent hook on the ball.

Curve-ball Delivery

The curve-ball delivery is not widely used and is not recommended for beginners. It is difficult to control because of its wide arc when traveling toward the pins and because of the difficulty in adjusting a curve-ball delivery to the varying degrees of slickness of different alleys. The curve ball (sometimes called the big looper or rainbow) is a relatively slow-moving ball with a counter-clockwise spin that takes effect sooner and thus produces a larger curve that acts for a longer period of time than is true for the hook ball.

Backup-ball (Reverse or Reverse-hook Ball) Delivery

Under no circumstances is the backup-ball delivery or variations recommended. For a right-handed bowler, a reverse ball is one that travels first toward the left and then curves to the right before hitting the pins. The backup ball is a poor strike-getter because it goes into the headpin pocket at a very slight angle, and the ball produces poor pin-mixing action. Few strikes, a disproportionate number of splits, and difficult pin leaves result when the backup ball is used. In addition, it is a difficult delivery to control consistently.

A backup ball results when one or more of the following occur:

(1) A lack of concentration when delivering the ball.

(2) Rotating the forearm in a clockwise direction or allowing the fingers to leave the ball first.

(3) The fingers are held too far under the ball during the carry, thus causing a clockwise rotation of the forearm during the release.

(4) The thumb hole is too tight; thus, the thumb comes out late and the thumb instead of the fingers imparts a lift to the ball.

WORK FOR CONSISTENCY

"Unchanging," "grooved," "automatic," "consistency"—these are words used to describe the beginnner's ultimate objective in applying himself to the fundamentals of bowling. The key to good bowling has been described as the ability to roll the strike ball the same way every time. The stance, arm swing, approach, and release must all be practiced and improved until the bowler can confidently step upon the runway, forget all details of the movement, begin the delivery, and be confident that the ball will be placed in the desired position on the alley bed and given the desired impetus. Developing this consistency in the bowling delivery means eliminating the slightest unwanted manipulation of the hand, the slightest miscalculation in taking the stance, or the smallest wavering of the body in approaching the foul line. This obviously puts a great premium on the so-called fundamentals, because without a consistent movement resulting in a consistent delivery, no one can be considered a really skilled bowler.

RULES

5

The official rules governing bowling are established by the American Bowling Congress and the Women's International Bowling Congress. The rules that are of importance to the casual bowler will be commented on here.

Legal Pinfall

Every ball delivered by the bowler counts unless it is declared a dead ball. Pins knocked down by another pin or pins rebounding from the side partition or rear cushion are counted as pins down. If, when the ball is rolled at a full set-up or at a spare, it is discovered immediately after the delivery of the ball that one or more pins are improperly set, the ball and resulting pinfall shall be counted. Each player must determine if the set-up is correct. Incorrectly set pins should be respotted before the ball is delivered. Pins that are knocked down by a fair ball and remain lying on the alley bed or in the gutters, or which lean so as to touch kickbacks or side partitions, are termed deadwood and counted as pins down and are removed before the next ball is bowled.

Illegal Pinfall

When any of the following incidents occurs the ball counts as a ball rolled, but pins knocked down do not count: (A) When pins are knocked down or displaced by a ball that leaves the alley before reaching the pins. (B) When a ball rebounds from the rear cushion. (C) When pins come in contact with the body, arms, or legs of a pinsetter and rebound. (D) When a standing pin falls because of removal of deadwood or is knocked down by a pinsetter or mechanical pinsetting equipment; it must be replaced on the pin spot marked on the pin deck where it originally stood before delivery of the ball. (E) When pins that are bowled off the alley bed rebound and remain standing on the alley bed. (F) When a foul is committed in delivering the ball.

Dead Ball

A ball shall be declared dead if any of the following circumstances occurs, in which case the ball shall not count. (The pins are respotted and the player bowls again.) (A) If after the player delivers his ball attention is immediately called to the fact that one or more pins were missing from the set-up. (B) When a pinspotter removes or interferes with any pin or pins before they stop rolling or before the ball reaches the pins. (C) When a player bowls on the wrong alley or out of turn. (D) When the player is interfered with by any person or a moving object as the ball is being delivered and before delivery is completed, he must immediately accept the resulting pinfall or demand that pins be respotted. (E) When any pins at which he is bowling are moved or knocked down in any manner as the ball is being delivered and before the ball reaches the pins. (F) When a player's ball comes in contact with any foreign obstacle.

Foul

Although the foul rule is frequently disregarded by the occasional bowler, it should be observed as soon as bowling practice is started. A foul is committed whenever the foot, hand, or any part of the body touches the alley bed, equipment, or any part of the building such as a wall, or if the toe of the foot extends over although not actually touching the foul line. In the event of a foul, no pins are counted, the pins are respotted, but the ball rolled does count. Therefore, if a foul occurs on the first ball rolled in a frame, the pins are respotted, and should the bowler knock down all ten pins on the second ball, it is scored as a spare.

Scoring

Knowing how to score the game is of concern to every bowler. The rules for scoring and a sample line are illustrated in Illustration 8.

Etiquette

Bowling has its own set of "rules" which are not a part of the official regulations but which govern the behavior of all bowlers—

HOW BOWLING IS SCORED

Ten frames is a game. There are two balls to a frame to knock down all the pins.

A **strike:** knocking down all the pins with the first ball delivered in any frame. A strike is marked with an X as shown to indicate a credit of ten pins. To strike earns a bonus of all pins knocked down by the next two balls in the next frame or frames.

A **spare:** knocking all the pins down with two balls. A spare is marked with a / as shown to indicate a credit of ten pins. A spare earns a bonus of the pins knocked down by the next ball in the following frame.

A **split:** knocking down some pins with the first ball in such a way that some are left standing with space between them. A split is marked with a circle as shown.

A split becomes a spare when the remaining pins are knocked down with the second ball. A / is drawn as shown.

An **error** occurs when all the pins are **not** knocked down with two balls. A – is marked as shown. An exception to the error: when a split is left after the first ball, it is marked as a split, and not as an error.

Frame	Pins down on. 1st ball	2nd ball	Say it is an	Mark it thus:	Score in each frame	Accumu-lative score is
1	4	2	ERROR	4̸2	6	6
2	5	3	SPLIT	5̣3	8	14
3	6	4	SPARE	6̸4	10+7	31
4	7	3	SPARE	7̸3	10+10	51
5	10	—	STRIKE	X	10+10+10	81
6	10	—	STRIKE	X	10+10+6	107
7	10	—	STRIKE	X	10+6+0	123
8	6	—	ERROR	6̸–	6	129
9	F	10	SPARE	F̸/̸10	10+9	148
10	9	1	SPARE	9̸/̸X	10+10	168
	10					

IT WOULD LOOK LIKE THIS ON THE SCORE SHEET:

4̸2	5̣3	6̸4	7̸3	X	X	X	6̸–	F̸/̸10	9̸/̸X
6	14	31	51	81	107	123	129	148	168

Illustration 8

the so-called "etiquette" of bowling. These should be observed at all times. Of primary importance is your behavior as you wait for your turn and finally take it. First, you should always be ready to take your turn. However, if a bowler on an adjoining alley is addressing the pins, do not take your ball off the rack until that bowler has begun his approach. If two bowlers address the pins simultaneously, the bowler on the right has precedence. Do not bowl a different ball for your second turn in a frame. This is double-balling. If there is a pin-setter in the pit he may be injured because he may not be prepared for the second ball.

You should always be properly equipped for bowling; in particular, all bowling establishments require that regular bowling shoes be worn. You should exercise care in the use of all equipment provided, such as balls, shoes, and the alleys themselves. Show a respect for the property of others.

Bowling etiquette may be summed up by saying that good manners are called for on the part of the bowler. Many details could be specified but these are unnecessary when it is recognized that the fundamental idea which underlies all of the code of etiquette is consideration of others. If thoughtfulness and common sense have guided the bowler's conduct, the rules of etiquette will have been observed.

TRAINING PROGRAM

The ultimate goal of every bowler is to roll the ball so that its contact with the pins produces an effective hit. An effective hit is one in which the ball contacts the pins at the desired point and results in maximum pin fall. In Chapter 4 the movement fundamentals underlying the ability to roll the ball effectively were described. In this chapter a program will be outlined that should make it possible for the beginner to improve his skill in bowling and thus produce the effective hit more frequently and consistently. A series of progressive steps are described and the beginner is advised to check his proficiency at each progressive step. Begin with the first and move through each succeeding step as slowly or as rapidly as progress indicates. By following these directions, the maximum value can be derived from the recommended program. The advanced bowler may profit from these suggestions as well as the beginner.

STEP ONE

The first step in the program is the development of an effective arm swing. Begin the practice of the arm swing by limiting the approach to a single but not more than two steps. By limiting the approach to one or two steps, it is possible to concentrate on the movement of the bowling arm without undue emphasis on the timing or the coordinating of the arm swing and the steps. Practice the arm swing with the one-step approach and release the ball as the slide is taken. Be sure that the arm swing has the desired straight forward and backward arc, that the same position is reached on the backswing each time, that the height reached on the backswing is adequate, and that the arm swing is executed without unnecessary strain. The arm swing must be consistent before any attempt is made to add the complete approach. The consistency with which the ball is delivered in this situation can be checked by concentrating on how the movement "feels." The goal should be to deliver the ball and be able to say, "that felt right."

One guide in developing this perception is to observe the speed with which the ball travels the length of the lane. The time required for the ball to travel the distance of 60 feet gives a direct indication of the speed of the ball; that is, the less time required, the greater the speed of the ball. The woman bowler should try to develop a delivery in which the ball travels the distance in just under three seconds. For men, the time should be about two and one-half seconds. The time can be recorded by using a stop watch or a watch with a sweep second hand. The time gives an indication of the consistency of the speed with which the ball is delivered, thereby reflecting the consistency of the arm swing—the goal in step one. It is preferable to do this practice without pins in order to concentrate on the arm movement. When the arm swing has become consistent, begin practicing step two.

STEP TWO

The complete approach is now added. The key point to observe in checking the timing is that the right arm and left leg are moving forward simultaneously just before and with the release of the ball. If this timing can be achieved in an approach having a fair amount of momentum, the approach and arm swing have been well-coordinate and the delivery should be smooth. Again, consistency is crucial, but it must be remembered that reasonable speed is also necessary. As in the one-step delivery, time the ball's course from the release to the arrival at the head pin area. With the complete approach, the time required for the ball to travel to the head pin area should now be reduced by about a quarter of a second. The goal for women is to deliver the ball so that it covers the distance in two and one-half to two and three-fourths seconds. For men, this time should be between two and two and one-half seconds. As a rule, champion bowlers roll at these speeds. This is also in accord with the caution—directed primarily at the men—not to throw the ball too fast. The above times are recommended on the basis of data gathered on league bowlers and on a study of the effects of variations in the speed of balls delivered to the 1-3 pocket. In this study, the times ranged from 2.5 to 6.0

seconds (less than 2.5 was impossible to achieve under the particular experimental conditions). It was found that balls in the 2.5 to 2.9 speed range had the highest percentage of strikes, 3.0 to 3.4 next, and so on.

The speed of the ball and the consistency of that speed reflect the achievement of the desired consistency in the movement and of a co-ordinated arm and swing and approach. The first phase, then, in developing a full delivery is to add the steps, delivering the ball a few times until the movement is freed from initial awkwardness— anywhere from a few to as many as a dozen or more deliveries. Let the pushaway initiate the approach and then forget the steps con-centrating on the free arm swing and on the timing of the movement just prior to and during the release of the ball. Do not spend too much time on this initial practice, but soon begin to observe the speed of the ball to evaluate the consistency of the approach and delivery. Keep the ball on the lane, but do not emphasize a greater degree of accuracy than that at this time. Bowling without the pins set up is still highly desirable at this stage. If the pins are set up, there is a tendency to pay more attention to knocking them down than to con-centrating on the movement. Many good bowlers strongly advocate bowling without pins until the fundamental skills have been de-veloped.

Suppose there is difficulty with the speed, consistency, or timing of the delivery. Inadequate speed can be caused by restricting the range of the arm swing. Check the height of the back swing to determine if the arm reaches a position parallel with the floor, and check that the ball is swung and not carried. A second point to note is the approach: the steps should result in increased momentum of the body when moving toward the foul line. The approach is made so that the body is moving faster at the beginning of the last step than at the completion of the first step. Should the delivery be too fast, applying the reverse of these two points—slowing down the approach and restricting the height of the backswing—should reduce the speed of the ball. Lack of consistency can be caused by a variation in the range or speed of the arm swing; a consistent arm swing should have been developed before the approach was added but it should now be rechecked. An inconsistent approach creates problems. Be sure that the starting position is taken exactly; practice the approach a few times without the ball. Finally, if the right arm and left leg do not move forward simultaneously during the last step, the approach has probably been started ahead of the arm swing. Try letting the pushaway pull you into the approach. A second fault is rushing the approach while moving toward the foul line. If this occurs, deliberately slow down the approach by concentrating on a walking speed.

Practice the full approach and arm swing until the release is correctly timed and the ball is delivered with a consistent speed that is within the recommended range. As soon as this goal has been achieved, begin concentrating on the delivery of the ball to the 1-3 pocket.

STEP THREE

It will be assumed at this point that either or both the straight ball and the natural-hook deliveries have been tried and that one of these has been chosen. In making this selection both deliveries were practiced so that now there is some notion of how the chosen delivery should be executed. The next step is to concentrate on where the ball crosses the foul line. A clear distinction is made here between the ball's position as it *crosses* the foul line and the release which should take place *after* the ball has crossed the foul line. If the lane is marked with the Brunswick Range Finder (see Illustration 9), the row of dots at the foul line is used to judge the position of the ball. If the lanes are not equipped with this device, judge the position of the ball by observing the board (counting from the right edge of the runway) over which the center of the ball passes. The bowler should not

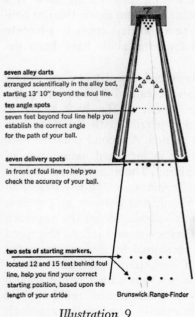

seven alley darts
arranged scientifically in the alley bed, starting 13' 10" beyond the foul line.

ten angle spots
seven feet beyond foul line help you establish the correct angle for the path of your ball.

seven delivery spots
in front of foul line to help you check the accuracy of your ball.

two sets of starting markers,
located 12 and 15 feet behind foul line, help you find your correct starting position, based upon the length of your stride

Brunswick Range-Finder

Illustration 9

attempt to judge this position; he should have another person make this observation. The bowler's attention will soon be directed to a point of aim and the entire concentration must be on that point and not on the position of the ball at the foul line. The objective here is to determine whether or not the ball crosses the foul line repeatedly at the same place from a given starting position. In order to have something at which to aim while practicing, watch the second alley dart (counting from the right). (See Illustration 9.) This aiming point may need adjustment later, but it will suffice for the present. Once a consistent release position has been achieved, the starting position can be adjusted, either to the right or the left, so that the ball can be released at the proper place for the type of ball delivery chosen. This degree of consistency in the release position is necessary to attain a high degree of skill.

A straight ball should be released between the first and second dots (about 7½ boards) from the right edge of the runway. Some adjustments from this may be made. For example, a release over the first dot is sometimes recommended. However, the release of the ball so that it crosses the foul line between the first and second dots enables the second alley dart to be used as the point of aim for a spot bowler. A release either to the right or left of the above necessitates a point of aim that is slightly to the right or left of the second alley dart and lacks some precision in aiming. A hook ball is released about midway between the right edge and the center of the lane. Because of the variability in the amount of hook obtained by hook-ball bowlers, the hook-ball bowler may need to make an adjustment in his release position, depending upon the amount of hook his ball takes.

Achieving a consistent release position is dependent upon an exact starting position. Use the range finder markings on the runway and mark the starting position to the nearest board right or left of a dot or on a dot. (See Illustration 9.) If the alley is not marked with the range finder, the starting position should be noted by counting the number of boards from the right edge and placing the feet in the same position each time.

The second factor that can affect the consistency of the release position is the direction of the approach. It has already been pointed out that the steps should be taken directly toward the foul line; be careful not to drift to the right or the left. A major problem for many right-handed beginners is the tendency to drift to the left, particularly if the pins are up. If the steps are not taken in a line perpendicular to the foul line, this will be obvious when the check is made on the spot at which the ball crosses the foul line.

Characteristically, the bowler who drifts is either inconsistent in his release or his ball is always released to the left or right of the desired position.

How can this be observed? This is somewhat difficult due to the size of the ball and the obvious need for almost pin-point precision at the foul line. The release position should be judged by observing where the center of the ball crosses the foul line, and this should be done specifically in terms of the number of boards to the right or left of the nearest dot. It is recommended that this be observed and recorded by a helper so that the record can be checked for a series of 10 or 20 deliveries in order to determine consistency and to identify errors. The written record of the release position may be made in several ways. The most obvious is to have the observer judge the ball's position and write down the number of boards to the right or left of the desired release position at which the ball crossed the foul line. A simpler method is to use a record sheet (See Illustration 14, page 56) in which the foul line area is sketched in and the ball's position can be clearly indicated for each of a series of deliveries. This type of record provides a clear and summarized picture of the consistency or lack of consistency in the release position. The same score sheet is also useful for checking other aspects of accuracy, and these will be commented on in subsequent sections.

How is this written record used? If, for a given number of deliveries, the record indicates that the ball is released over the second dot while attempting to release between the first and second dots, two possible errors may have occurred.

The first check point should be the tendency to drift to one side. If an observer stands behind the bowler, he should be able to detect this. The correction of the fault may be difficult, but one remedy is to concentrate on walking straight ahead. A second aid is to mark the runway with chalk or masking tape as a guide for the approach. Finally, it may even be necessary to over-correct by concentrating on walking slightly to the opposite side.

The second factor to check is the starting position. Suppose the ball is consistently released three boards to the left of the desired release position. Moving the starting position three boards to the right may correct the error in the release position.

Another common error is the failure to keep the shoulders and hips squarely facing the pin area at the time of release. This can be readily observed since there is a tendency to bring the rear leg around the body toward the left when the error is committed. To correct this fault, keep the shoulders squarely facing the pins throughout the approach and release, and use the rear foot to provide better balance and to help prevent turning of the body by keeping it in contact with the runway during the slide.

This stage of developing bowling skill may be difficult. It is important to develop a delivery in which the ball position deviates no more than one board to the right or left of the desired release point. Do not cut this practice time short. It provides an opportunity to further perfect the approach, the ball delivery is being practiced, and, above all, a crucial goal in bowling will be achieved when the ball is released at the same place beyond the foul line on each delivery.

During this practice of the release position, continue observing the path of the ball. For those who bowl a straight ball, this is helpful in noting any tendency to develop a back-up ball. If detected, this should be corrected immediately. Concentrate on the hand position recommended for the straight ball—thumb held in the 11 or 12 o'clock position throughout the delivery. For the hook bowler, this practice provides an opportunity to observe the consistency of the hook and the amount of break in the ball. If the hook is consistent, this practice allows the best release position to be found.

STEP FOUR

The fourth step is developing the "strike-ball" path. The bowler should now be ready to direct his full attention to knocking down pins and, hence, must decide whether to pin or spot bowl. When pin bowling, look at the pins during the delivery and attempt to have the ball hit the 1-3 pocket. For any set-up other than all 10 pins, the desired place for the ball to hit the pins is identified and that becomes the point of aim. When spot bowling, look at a spot on the lane over which the ball should pass on its way to the pins. In most of the literature on bowling, pin powling is recommended for the beginner, whereas spot bowling is reserved for those more advanced in skill. In a study of college women bowlers, there was a significant difference in achievement scores in favor of those taught the spot point of aim. This suggests that the beginner can spot bowl immediately. The advantage of spot bowling is that the point of aim is located about one-third of the distance to the pins, making it easier to hit the point of aim. There is little doubt that spot bowling eventually adds to the precision of almost all bowlers.

Since the desired point of contact at the pins will be commented on in the discussion of picking up spares, and since the pin bowler aims at this point, no further comment in this section will be made concerning pin bowling. The subsequent discussion will be concerned with the desired spot at which the ball should be directed.

The strike ball (bowling at the 1-3 pocket) is delivered at least 50 per cent of the time in any game. Therefore, it is important to concentrate on perfecting this aspect of the game. These comments are directed to the straight-ball bowler. The desired release point is between the first and second dots and the point of aim will be the second dart from the right. If an adjustment was made in the release position, another will now have to be made in the point of aim. The adjustment will vary with each individual. Study the range-finder diagram and figure out where the adjusted point of aim should be. The release position and the point of aim form a direct line to the 1-3 pocket. The reason for developing a consistent release should now be obvious. The two marks or spots form a line to the pocket and any deviation of ball placement with respect to either mark will cause the ball to miss, to some degree, the 1-3 pocket. At this point, therefore, a check point on accuracy is being added. Continue to observe the relationship of the ball to the dart as well as the relationship of the ball to the desired release point. The question of bowling at the pins now arises. It would be desirable to direct attention to perfecting the ability to hit the dot (or board) and the dart (or board) before actually bowling at any pins. How long this practice should continue is difficult to assess. Some practice in observing the ball relationship to the dot and dart is useful before bowling at pins. This not only serves to focus attention on the point of aim but provides a further check on the release position.

The hook-ball bowler should follow the same procedures except that the initial point of aim is a dart, or board, in line with the release position. The desired path of the hook ball is a straight one from the dot or board at the foul line over the dart or board directly in line with the release board or dot after which the ball begins its "break" and hooks into the pocket.

Up to this point all the suggestions to the spot bowler concerning the point of aim have been made relative to the range finder. If the lanes are not equipped with this device, the division boards may be substituted for use in spot bowling. The division boards are interspliced light and dark colored boards located twenty feet from the foul line. For example, the fifth dark board from the right edge of the alley bed is approximately in line with the second alley dart in the range finder system and can be substituted for that spot. Similarly, the hook bowler can find his spot using the division boards as marks.

The pins should now be set up. When first bowling at the pins, it is recommended that less than 10 pins be the target. It is highly desirable to focus attention on hitting the 1-3 pocket—not on how many pins have been knocked down. A set-up such the 1-2-3-5-6 is good for this purpose. This provides an opportunity to observe small deviations from the point of contact; that is, the ball hits the 1-3, or the 1, or the 1-2, or the 2 pin indicating progressive deviations to the left of the desired contact point. Similarly, deviations to the right can be observed. Setting up the 5 pin provides an opportunity to observe whether or not the 1-3 pocket hit was such that it would carry the 5 pin, which must be done if the hit is to be a strike. Some balls hitting the pocket will not knock down the 5 pin. Thus the following hits can be observed: a 1-3 pocket hit which carries the 5 pin (the desired objective), a 1-3 pocket hit which does not carry the 5 pin (pretty good for the beginner), and deviations to the right or left of the desired point of contact. This practice does not give emphasis to the number of pins knocked down (for example, a hit in the 1-2 pocket may be a strike but it is not indicative of precision on the part of the right-handed bowler). Bowling at a set-up such as 1-2-3-5-6 puts the premium on hitting the 1-3 pocket.

As in the development of the consistent release point, the relationship of the ball to the dart should be observed and recorded by the bowler. This is essential in developing accuracy. A major fault of the beginner is looking away from the point of aim to soon. The spot bowler should always keep his eyes on the point of aim—a dart or some board relative to the dart—until the ball has crossed that part of the lane. The pin bowler keeps his eyes on the pocket until the ball has hit its mark. Using the check sheet previously mentioned (see Illustration 14, page 56) record by how many boards the point of aim was missed and whether to the right or left. As before, the center of the ball must pass over the desired spot. The ball contact with the pins should also be recorded on the same sheet: 1-3 (circled to indicate that the 5 pin was carried), 1-3 (not circled if the 5 pin does not fall), 1, 1-2, 2, 3, 3-6, 6. Thus, the record is complete and indicates the exact line which the ball followed from the release to to pin contact. This practice should be continued until a fair degree of consistency has been achieved. The decision of how long to continue will depend upon the time available and the persistency of the bowler. Regardless of the amount of time spent at this stage, continue in all subsequent bowling to direct attention to perfecting the line to the 1-3 pocket. Any ball rolled at the 1-3 pocket should be observed for possible errors in the release, point of aim, and point of contact.

An inability to get the ball to roll over the aiming spot may be due to not keeping the eyes on the spot. This is the first check point when practicing. The need for a straight forward arc was stressed when the development of the arm swing was discussed. The reason should now be apparent. Any deviation in the arc of the swing will produce problems in getting the ball to roll over the desired spot. The desirability of keeping the shoulders squarely facing the pins has also been stressed a number of times. This is another check point for this aspect of accuracy. Any rotation of the body as the ball is released may cause a change in the direction of the ball's path. Poor coordination of the arm swing and the approach is often the cause of turning the body during the release. To summarize, the initial stress placed on developing a good arm swing, a straight approach, and effectively coordinating these two aspects are the basic fundamentals which, when mastered, enable an accurate delivery to be made. Bowl-

ing at pins can be an unhappy experience if these have not been
developed to the degree that consistency is evident.

STEP FIVE

The fifth step is acquiring skill in picking up spares. Practice spare
bowling at every opportunity. With experience, a bowler will find
that his type and speed of delivery tend to cause only a few common
spare set-ups to be left. By maintaining actual records of the spare
leaves, a bowler will soon learn which spares will most likely occur
in actual game situations. Naturally, these are the spare set-ups on
which practice time should be spent. Right-handed bowlers are particularly urged to practice rolling at the number 10 pin since this
is a frequent leave and commonly causes difficulty for a good many
right-handed bowlers.

A strike hit has to be relatively accurate in order to knock down
all ten pins. In most instances, a spare hit can be less accurate and
still knock down the remaining pins. When only one pin remains
standing, the bowler actually has a larger target than is commonly
realized. The target area is not just a pin that is almost five inches
in diameter at the height at which it is struck by the ball, but
includes, in addition, the full width of the ball to the left and to
the right of the pin.

Do not change the type of delivery for spare shots but use the
same delivery as for the strike ball. An effective spare shot also
depends upon establishing the desired line for the delivery and then
being able to deliver the ball upon this line. The spare pick-up line
consists of the release spot, the point of aim, and the ball-pin contact
point. Obviously, there are a number of these lines to consider in
spare bowling; the actual line depends upon the number of pins
standing and their relationship to each other.

The first problem is the identification of the desired ball-pin contact. When a single pin remains standing, deliver the ball so that its
center contacts the center of the pin. This point of contact allows
for the greatest margin of error to either side. When two or more
pins remain standing, however, the ball will be deflected by its first
pin contact and this deflection must be taken into account. The
amount of deflection depends upon the speed of the ball, the weight

of the pins, and the angle at which the pin or pins are contacted. Consequently, to some extent, this is somewhat of a special problem for each bowler. A few general suggestions can be made that apply to most bowlers and these will be discussed specifically for given spares.

Once the desired point of contact has been specified, it remains only to identify the most effective release position and the point of aim. A basic rule which utilizes maximum alley angle has been suggested by a number of star bowlers and teachers of bowling. This serves as one general guide. When the pin or pins that remain standing are on the left-hand side of the lane, the ball should be delivered from the right-hand side, and, conversely, when the spare is on the right-hand side, the ball should be started to the left of the release position for the strike ball. Following this general rule, the spot bowler will pick up all spare leaves on the left side from approximately the strike-ball release position (some slight modifications may be necessary) with the major change made in the point of aim. For spares on the right-hand side, the spot bowler releases the ball somewhere on the left half of the runway and again changes the point of aim. The specific release positions and points of aim following this system will be discussed for particular spares. The same basic rule of maximum alley angle applies for the pin bowler as well.

There is, however, another system that has been used with success by some women bowlers. This system is based on the principle that the line used for the strike ball can be used for spare leaves on the left side of the alley by releasing the ball to the left of the release position and adjusting the point of aim accordingly.

For example, if the desired point of contact at the pins is the 1-2 pocket (used for the 1-3-6-8-10 spare), move the starting position five boards to the left, release the ball at the foul line five boards to the left of the strike ball release position, and roll the ball over the third alley dart if bowling a straight ball. If bowling a hook, the same shift is made in the starting position and release, and the point of aim is moved to the left an equivalent distance. Thus, a line which is parallel to that used for the strike ball is used for spare set-ups on the left side. This makes it possible to utilize the consistent delivery of the strike ball to pick up particular spares. For spare leaves on the right-hand side of the alley, the bowler identifies a straight line to the given spare which is parallel to the alley bed and bowls this line. This may seem to present a mental hazard, but many women bowlers actually prefer this line. Women bowlers using this system have been as successful in picking up spares as have women bowlers using the maximum alley angle system. It is recommended that first both systems be tried and then a choice made. A combination of the two systems may be used. Here, the maximum angle is used for spare leaves on the right side, while the strike-ball line is maintained for spares on the left side. Additional details about each system will be given as suggestions for picking up specific spares are made.

The problem of picking up spares can be simplified somewhat if a number of groupings of spare leaves are identified for which a given ball-pin contact is effective in carrying all of the pins of a given set-up. Some divergence of opinion exists concerning the most effective ball-pin contact for some spares, but there is more agreement than disagreement for most spares. Some of the common groupings as well as individual problem spares will be presented, and, wherever possible, a suggested ball-pin contact and the desired line of the ball for both systems of spare pick-ups will be given. No comments will be made on the desired path for the hook ball since this is an individual problem that depends upon the amount of hook on the ball. Picking up spares on the left side involves a systematic shift to the left for the hook-ball bowler, particularly for the system that is based on utilizing the strike-ball delivery. The amount of shift is the same as that for the straight-ball bowler, that is, five boards to the left for each new pocket (the 1-2, 2-4), and two and one-half boards for a shift of one half of a pocket such as to the 1 pin from the 1-3 pocket.

The 1-3 pocket ball. The same line which is used for the strike ball can be used to cover the 1, 3, 5, 5-8, 1-2-5, 1-2-9, 1-2-4-7-9, and possibly a few other spare leaves in the right-center area. For these spares no change is made in the delivery under either system of spare pick-ups.

The 1-2 pocket ball. A ball rolled at the 1-2 pocket will carry the 2, 8, 2-8, 5-9, 1-2-8, 1-3-8, 2-4-5, 2-4-5-8, and 1-3-6-8-10 spare leaves. To roll the ball at this pocket when using the maximum alley angle system, keep the release position the same as that for the strike ball but roll the ball between the second and third alley darts. For the strike-ball system, release the ball between the second and third dots and roll it over the third alley dart from the right (see Illustration 10).

The 2-4 pocket ball. If the 4, 7, 4-7, 4-7-8, 2-4-7, 2-7, or the 7-8 pins remain standing, the ball-pin contact is the 2-4 pocket. The line to pick up these spares using the maximum alley angle system is from the first alley dot over a spot just slightly to the right of the third alley dart (see Illustration 11). To use the system which capitalizes

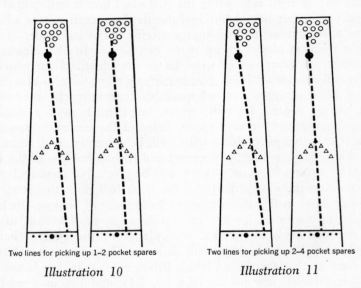

Two lines for picking up 1-2 pocket spares   Two lines for picking up 2-4 pocket spares

Illustration 10   *Illustration 11*

on the strike-ball delivery pattern, release the ball so that it crosses the foul line between the third and fourth dots and goes over the fourth (or center alley) dart (see Illustration 11).

The 3-6 pocket ball. This ball-pin contact will carry the 6, 10, 6-10, 6-9-10, 3-6-10, and the 3-10 spares when using the maximum alley angle system. Release the ball at the second dot from the left-hand side and roll it between the third and fourth alley darts counting from the left (see Illustration 12). These same spares can be covered in the strike-ball system by substituting the 6 pin as the ball-pin contact. Deliver the ball over the second dot and second alley dart from the right-hand side. This line is parallel to the side of the alley.

Some problem spares. The 3-9 tandem leave—with one pin directly behind the other (also called a sleeper)—can usually be made only if the ball contacts the 3 pin squarely. Any other hit causes the ball and the 3 pin to be deflected and both miss the 9 pin. The most advantageous line for this spare is to roll the ball over the third dot and the third alley dart counting from the right; this is a line parallel to the alley which carries the straight ball squarely into the 3 pin (see Illustration 13). The hook-ball bowler will find it more advan-

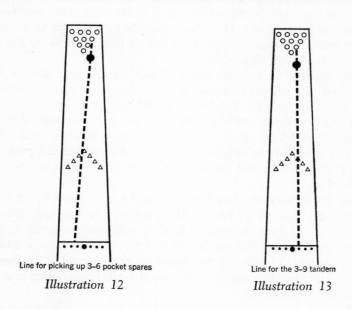

Line for picking up 3–6 pocket spares

Illustration 12

Line for the 3–9 tandem

Illustration 13

tageous to release the ball from the left-hand side and roll the ball cross-alley so that it will hook back squarely into the 3 pin.

Picking up splits is a problem faced by all bowlers. Some general guides to follow will be illustrated by applying them to specific spares. For example, the only way to convert the 5-7 is to have the ball strike the 5 pin on the right side and deflect the 5 pin so that it carries the 7 pin. Conversely, the 5-10 is converted by having the ball strike the 5 pin on the left side causing the 5 pin to strike the 10 pin. Thus, the front pin is contacted on the side opposite to the direction in which the pin must travel toward the back pin. This is true for so-called wide splits and applies also to set-ups in which the pins stand side-by-side. The side-by-side wide splits are much more difficult to pick up since they require an extremely thin ball-pin contact so that the pin aimed at will be deflected not backward and to the side as in the 5-7 but, rather, almost directly sideward. Use this technique for the 4-6 and similar set-ups, all of which are extremely difficult to convert.

Other splits in which the pins stand side-by-side, but in which the ball could not pass between the pins as in the wide splits, include the 4-5 and similar set-ups. Here the principle to follow is to have the ball contact the exact center of the set-up (for example, in the case of the 4-5, a direct "2-pin" hit).

The so-called baby splits, the 3-10 and the 2-7, have already been discussed, the desired ball-pin contact being the 3-6 (or 6) and the 2-4, respectively. This suggestion would appear to be inconsistent with the comments made for the 5-7 and 5-10, although the technique suggested for these is applied by some bowlers to the baby splits. The advantage of using the 3-6 (or 6) and the 2-4 pockets is that if the spare is not converted, at least one pin is carried most of the time.

The importance of spare bowling cannot be overemphasized. If a spare is made in all 10 frames, then, without getting any strikes at all, a score of 170 or 180 is possible. If, in addition to converting most of the spare leaves, three or four strikes are also obtained, a score of 200 is feasible. That this is an important achievement is emphasized by the fact that less than one thousand male bowlers last year had a league average of 200.

GLOSSARY 7

ABC. American Bowling Congress, the governing body for organized bowling in the United States.

Alley. The wooden lane on which the ball is delivered. Also, the name used to designate the building in which one can bowl.

Anchor. The last player to bowl for a bowling team.

Approach. The area between the front of the lane and the foul line on which the delivery is made. This area is commonly called the runway. The footwork and style used by a bowler when delivering the ball is also termed an approach.

Baby split. A split in which only the 2 and 7 pins or the 3 and 10 pins remain standing after the first ball in a frame has hit the pins.

Back-up ball. A ball which, when rolling down the alley, curves toward the side of the bowler's body from which it was delivered. For a right-handed bowler, a back-up ball curves to the right. A reverse ball.

Ball rack. The rack on the side of the alley approach to which the bowling balls are returned on the track from the alley pit and on which the bowlers' balls are stored between turns.

Bed posts. A split in which only the 7 and 10 pins remain standing. Also called *fence posts, goal posts,* or the *7-10 railroad.*

Big four. A split in which the 4, 6, 7, and 10 pins remain standing. Also termed a *4-6-7-10 split* or *big ears.*

Blow. Failure to knock down the remaining pins with the second ball when there is not a split. An error.

Brooklyn. Hitting the side of the head pin (number 1 pin) opposite that side of the body from which the ball was delivered. For a right-handed bowler, this is the 1-2 pocket. Also called a *crossover.* In New York, this is termed a *Jersey.*

Cherry. Knocking down the front pin or pins on a spare set-up but leaving the back pin(s) standing. Also called a *chop.*

Count. The number of pins knocked down by the first ball delivered after a spare has been made. This is sometimes called a *bill* in the Eastern United States.

Cross-alley shot. A ball which crosses the center of the alley on its way to the pins. Sometimes used to designate a ball delivered from the extreme corner of the alley.

Crossover. A ball which hits on the side of the head pin opposite from the side of the body from which delivered. A *Brooklyn.*

Curve ball. For a right-handed bowler, the ball which travels toward the right edge of the alley and then curves or breaks in toward the center of the alley before hitting the pins.

Deadball. An ineffective ball that does not mix the pins.

Division boards. That area on the alley where the light- and dark-colored boards intersect.

Double. Two successive strikes in a game.

Double balling. Rolling a second ball at the pins before the first ball has been returned.

Dutch 200 or dutchman. A 200 score made by alternating strikes and spares for the entire ten frames.

Error. Failure to make a spare when there is no split. A *blow* or *miss.*

Fast lane. A highly-polished alley bed which resists the hooking or curving action of the ball. In some localities, this condition is described as a *slow lane,* or a *"holding" alley.*

Foundation. A strike made in the ninth frame.

Foul. A rule infraction (usually touching or going beyond the foul line) for which the bowler is penalized by the loss of the pins downed on that roll.

Foul line. The black line separating the runway and the actual beginning of the alley or lane. A bowler touching or going beyond the foul line during his delivery has committed a foul.

Frame. Tenth part of a game indicated by each of the ten large squares on the score sheet.

Full hit. A ball that strikes the target pin at or near its center.

Grip. The method of grasping the ball during the delivery.

Gutter. A hollow trough on either side of the alley bed that catches the ball whenever it rolls off the side of the alley bed. The channel.

Handicap. A bonus score or score adjustment based on the difference between individual or team averages.

Head pin. The number one pin.

High hit. Hitting a pin head-on or squarely.

Hook. A delivery that travels in a straight line down the alley for about one-half to two-thirds of the distance and then curves sharply away from the side of the body from which delivered. For a right-handed bowler a hook ball breaks to the left as it nears the pins.

Inning. Each bowler's turn during the game. A *frame.*

King pin. The number 5 pin in some localities and the head pin in others.

Lane. The wooden playing surface on which the ball is rolled. That portion of the alley between the foul line and the pit. Another name for alley bed. Also called the *alley.*

Leave. The pin or pins that remain standing after the first ball has been delivered.

Lift. Imparting an upward motion to the ball with the fingers as the ball is released.

Light hit. Not hitting the target pin fully or squarely. A low or thin hit.

Line. A game or ten frames.

Lofting. Releasing the ball some distance above the alley and, consequently, throwing it some distance beyond the foul line during the delivery.

Mark. To make a strike or a spare.

Open frame. A frame without a mark (at least one pin remains standing after two balls have been delivered).

Pit. The space behind the alley bed into which the pins fall or roll when struck by the ball.

Pitch. The angle at which the finger and thumb holes are drilled into the bowling ball.

Pocket. The space between any two pins; most commonly used in references to the 1-3 or 1-2 pins.

Roundhouse. A curve ball with a wide curve. *Big looper.*

Runway. The space between the front of the lane and the foul line on which the delivery is made.

Sleeper. A pin that is hidden behind another pin and which is not readily seen from the runway.

Slow lane. A lane on which the ball readily hooks or curves. A *running alley.* The opposite meaning is given to this term in some localities.

Spare. Knocking down all the remaining pins with the second ball in a frame.

Split. Two or more pins remain standing after the first ball has been delivered; the number one pin has fallen and at least one pin is down between or ahead of the remaining pins.

Spot. A mark or location on the lane at which the bowler aims during the delivery.

Steal. A term applied when more pins fall than the amount deserved in view of the type of hit made.

Strike. Knocking down all of the pins with the first ball in any frame.

Striking out. Getting three strikes in the last frame or striking to the completion of the game.

Thin hit. Barely hitting the target pin.

Turkey. Hitting three successive strikes during a game. Also called a triple.

Working ball. A ball with a lot of spin that mixes the pins and causes a good pin fall.

SELF-TESTING
AND EVALUATION

The techniques included in this chapter provide for the evaluation of several aspects of bowling. First, devices and methods for assessing performance in the actual delivery of the ball will be suggested. These include techniques for observation of the release position, point of aim, type of delivery, ball-pin contact, and speed of the ball. Second, attention will be directed to assessing the results of the delivery including such items as the effectiveness of the strike ball delivery, effectiveness in converting spares, and the game score itself. Finally, a list of questions will be presented which test understanding of and knowledge about bowling. These self-evaluation devices are intended to be used as aids to learning and not merely as tests of final performance.

Assessing the Delivery

Some of the procedures recommended for observing and evaluating achievement in the various aspects of the ball delivery have been mentioned in previous sections. The importance of employing these techniques to help improve performance was stressed. (It might be helpful to re-read some of the material in Chapter 6 at this time.) The importance of consistency in the speed and accuracy of the delivery of the ball has been commented on throughout this booklet. Self-testing methods such as those suggested here make it possible to determine the degree to which this consistency of performance is being achieved as bowling skills improve.

For evaluating the delivery, the use of a chart such as that given in Illustration 14 is recommended. Note that the chart includes a system for determining the release position. This is done by recording the precise point at which the center of the ball passes over the foul line. The chart is designed for use with the Brunswick Range Finder, but a similar chart could be constructed showing the foul line area without the dots and used in much the same way. To use the chart, first indicate the expected release position above the column labeled "Release Point" by placing an "X" directly over that point at the top of the column.

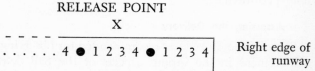

Release Point	Point of Aim	Pocket Hit	Path of Ball	Pins Down
1234·1234·1234·1234·1234·1234·1234·1234	1234▲1234▲1234▲1234▲1234▲1234▲1234		↑ ↖ ↗	
1234·1234·1234·1234·1234·1234·1234·1234	1234▲1234▲1234▲1234▲1234▲1234▲1234		↑ ↖ ↗	
1234·1234·1234·1234·1234·1234·1234·1234	1234▲1234▲1234▲1234▲1234▲1234▲1234		↑ ↖ ↗	
1234·1234·1234·1234·1234·1234·1234·1234	1234▲1234▲1234▲1234▲1234▲1234▲1234		↑ ↖ ↗	
1234·1234·1234·1234·1234·1234·1234·1234	1234▲1234▲1234▲1234▲1234▲1234▲1234		↑ ↖ ↗	
1234·1234·1234·1234·1234·1234·1234·1234	1234▲1234▲1234▲1234▲1234▲1234▲1234		↑ ↖ ↗	
1234·1234·1234·1234·1234·1234·1234·1234	1234▲1234▲1234▲1234▲1234▲1234▲1234		↑ ↖ ↗	
1234·1234·1234·1234·1234·1234·1234·1234	1234▲1234▲1234▲1234▲1234▲1234▲1234		↑ ↖ ↗	
1234·1234·1234·1234·1234·1234·1234·1234	1234▲1234▲1234▲1234▲1234▲1234▲1234		↑ ↖ ↗	
1234·1234·1234·1234·1234·1234·1234·1234	1234▲1234▲1234▲1234▲1234▲1234▲1234		↑ ↖ ↗	

Illustration 14

For example, suppose you are a straight-ball bowler using the line recommended in the range finder system—release between dots 1 and 2. An "X" is marked between the numbers 2 and 3 located between dots 1 and 2, counting from the right. This is midway between dots 1 and 2. Thus:

RELEASE POINT

X

· · · · · · 4 ● 1 2 3 4 ● 1 2 3 4 | Right edge of runway

Now a helper observes the actual position of the ball in passing over the foul line as you make your delivery. This position is then recorded on the chart by drawing in a heavy vertical line in the first row of dots and numbers of the column. Thus:

RELEASE POINT

X

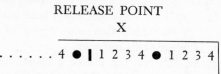

· · · · · · 4 ● | 1 2 3 4 ● 1 2 3 4

On this first delivery, you did not achieve the expected release position. It is advisable to make the necessary adjustments only after a series of deliveries have been made so that the "pattern" of release is evident.

Should you release consistently to the left, say by two boards, two choices are open to you. One, adjust the starting position or approach as needed to make the correction. Or, two, you might decide to establish a line to the 1-3 pocket according to the new, consistent, release position. The latter choice should be made only if the release is consistent and if it is not too near the center of the alley.

The chart also contains a place on which to record the position of the center of the ball as it passes the point of aim. This second type of evaluation is omitted by the pin bowler since the line in pin bowling includes only two items, the release and the ball-pin contact. As this is observed and recorded, your attention is focused on the accuracy with which you can deliver the ball over the chosen spot. In using the chart, again mark your expected point of aim (for the release position between dots 1 and 2, bowl over the second dart from the right). Thus:

POINT OF AIM

X

```
- -  _____
... 1 2 3 4 ▲ 1 2 3 4 ▲ 1 2 3 4 |  Right edge of
                                 |    alley bed
```

Now deliver the ball and observe where its center crosses the area on the alley bed where the darts are placed. Suppose that on the first delivery, the ball crosses over the second dart. Mark the chart in the first row in this manner:

POINT OF AIM

X

```
- - - _____
.... 1 2 3 4⚑1 2 3 4 ▲ 1 2 3 4|
```

The third check point is the ball-pin contact. This should also be recorded for each delivery of the ball, since the relationship of the three check points determines the line of the ball. All must be checked and perhaps corrected in order to attain a high degree of precision. Under the column headed "Pocket Hit" record the pin or pins which the ball actually contacts; for instance, the 1, 1-3, 2, or the 1-2.

The last observation recorded on this chart is the type of ball delivery made. The path of the ball is observed and the appropriate delivery type is circled. This is recorded as straight, hook, back-up, or curve and is primarily for the beginner so that any deviation from the intended type of delivery is immediately noted.

Check the Speed

A check on the speed of the ball as indicated by the time it takes the ball to cover the distance from the foul line to the pins is also suggested. In the initial stages of developing bowling skill, the speed or time should be observed for as many deliveries as is possible. When bowling at pins, check the time frequently to avoid unintentional and excessive *slowing down* or *speeding up* of the ball. No less than a weekly check is recommended.

Check Total Score

When first beginning to bowl a series of lines (in which continued emphasis is placed on improving bowling skill), a number of items can be charted for the purpose of observing progress in the results of the ball delivery. The primary concern is for the end result—the actual game score. However, during one session of bowling an experienced (or advanced) bowler will show a great variation in his game scores. The score for any one game does not indicate with any certainty the level of skill. The scores for a number of lines must be averaged before a true picture of ability level will be evident. In a study of bowling norms and learning curves for college women, an average of five and ten lines was used to indicate initial and final performance level. This report contains norms which can be used to judge the amount of improvement made by a college woman (see reference number 7). It is recommended that the scores of all games bowled each week be averaged in order to determine the week-by-week progress in game score.

Check First Ball Average

Although you are primarily interested in your game scores, components of the total game can be identified and charted and may serve to identify problems in accuracy. For example, recording the number of pins knocked down on the first ball in each frame, adding these up for 10 frames, and then computing the first ball average is a method of determining the degree of accuracy in rolling the strike ball. Again, the first ball scores can be averaged to obtain a weekly record for the profile chart.

Check Ability to Pick Up Spares

Ability to pick up spares is another component of the total game score. A simple check system is to count the number of errors made per line, average the error scores for the week, and then chart the weekly average. A second aspect of evaluating ability to pick up spares is to observe the frequency with which particular spare leaves are occurring and which you do not make. This helps identify problem spares on which additional practice is needed. A final method for evaluating effectiveness in spare bowling is to chart the second ball percentage. For this you need (1) your first ball total pin fall for 10 frames (which was obtained in computing the first ball average) and (2) a record of the number of pins knocked down with the second ball. If all pins of the spare are carried, the spare mark will give the count. If you pick up some of the pins remaining but not all, write down the number knocked down. Then the first ball total (for ten frames only) substracted from 100 indicates the number of pins it was possible for you to pick up. Divide this number into the number of pins actually knocked down with the second ball and you have the second ball percentage. The second ball percentage does give some indication of your ability in spare bowling. Again chart weekly. (See Illustration 15.)

Profile of Bowling Achievement

Week	Average time for ball to travel from foul line to pins	Bowling average	Average number of pins knocked down on first ball	Average number of errors per line	Second ball percentage

Illustration 15

Check Knowledge of Bowling

The following list of questions is included so that you can test your knowledge of bowling.

1. What is the strike pocket for the left-handed bowler?
2. How many check points does a spot bowler use?
3. How many check points does a pin bowler use?
4. If two persons are bowling on adjacent lanes and all ten pins are set up on both alleys, which bowler bowls first?
5. When a bowler gets a strike in the tenth frame, how many (if any) more balls does he throw?
6. When a foul is committed during the delivery of the first ball in a frame, how is the score determined for that frame?
7. When a bowler gets a spare in the tenth frame, how many (if any) more balls does he throw?
8. What is the term used to designate the making of two strikes in succession?
9. What two terms are used to designate the making of three strikes in succession?
10. What is the most difficult split of all to pick up?
11. What type of hit is usually necessary to pick up a sleeper?
12. Where should the ball be released on the alley in relation to the foul line?
13. Where should a bowler aim his second ball if he has a 5-10 split?
14. Where should a bowler aim his second ball if he has a 2-7 split?
15. What organization is responsible for the rules of bowling?
16. What is the minimum number of times a bowler would have to deliver the ball to complete a game if he makes a strike in each frame?
17. How many times would a bowler deliver the ball to finish a game in which he never made a mark?
18. In delivering the ball, the bowler loses his balance and places one hand on the alley beyond the foul line. However, he does not touch the foul line so the foul light does not operate. Is this a foul?
19. How much distance should separate the palm of the hand from the surface of the bowling ball when the ball is fitted correctly?
20. What delivery is considered to be the most effective?

21. What is the best rule to follow to ensure that the arm swing and the approach are properly timed?

22. Approximately how many years has the game of ten-pin bowling been in existence?

23. For what purpose was the American Bowling Congress organized?

24. What rule best describes the height to which the backswing should be carried?

25. What advantage is gained by a right-handed bowler who centers the ball on the right shoulder when in the stance?

26. What two rules are recommended when performing the push-away phase of the arm swing?

BIBLIOGRAPHY

American Association for Health, Physical Education, and Recreation, Division of Girls' and Women's Sports. *Bowling-Fencing-Golf Guide, June 1958–June 1960*. Washington, D.C.: The Association, 1958. 128 pp.

American Bowling Congress. *Bowler's Manual*. Milwaukee: The Congress, 1939. 43 pp.

Day, Ned. *How to Bowl Better*. New York: Arco Publishing Co., 1960. 144 pp.

Fraley, Oscar. *The Complete Handbook of Bowling*. Englewood Cliffs, N.J.: Prentice-Hall, 1958. 133 pp.

How to Add X Pins to Your Bowling Score. (adapted from the AMF Guide to Natural Bowling.) New York: 1959. 16 pp.

Kalman, Victor (Editor). *Guide to Natural Bowling*. New York: Permabooks, 1959. 130 pp.

Phillips, Marjorie, and Dean Summers. "Bowling Norms and Learning Curves for College Women," *Research Quarterly*, 21: pp. 377-385, 1950.

Wilman, Joe. *Better Bowling*. New York: The Ronald Press Co., 1953. 96 pp.

Women's International Bowling Congress. *Bowler's Manual*. Columbus, Ohio: The Congress, 1942. 40 pp.